Unusual Pets

PYGMY GOATS

MARYSA STORM

BLACK RABBIT BOOKS

Bolt is published by Black Rabbit Books
P.O. Box 227, Mankato, Minnesota, 56002.
www.blackrabbitbooks.com

Alissa Thielges, editor; Rhea Magaro, designer and photo researcher

Library of Congress Cataloging-in-Publication Data
Names: Storm, Marysa, author.
Title: Pygmy goats / by Marysa Storm.
Description: Mankato, MN: Black Rabbit Books, [2026] | Series: Unusual pets | Includes bibliographical references and index. | Audience: Ages 8-12 | Audience: Grades 4-6
Identifiers: LCCN 2024043405 (print) | LCCN 2024043406 (ebook) | ISBN 9781644667811 (library binding) | ISBN 9781644667934 (ebook)
Subjects: LCSH: Pygmy goat—Juvenile literature. | Pygmy goats as pets—Juvenile literature.
Classification: LCC SF386.P94 S76 2026 (print) | LCC SF386.P94 (ebook) | DDC 636.3/9—dc23/eng/20241219
LC record available at https://lccn.loc.gov/2024043405

Image Credits

Alamy Stock Photo/Andrew Wilson, 4–5, 20–21, Farlap, 1, imageBROKER/David & Micha Sheldon, 10–11, Mark J. Barrett, 9; Dreamstime/Bernard Bialorucki, 3, Lee Dawe, 26; Getty Images/retales botijero, 6–7; Shutterstock/Amanda Lakotish, 16 (middle), Bailey Davenport, 23 (bottom), Dipak Talati, 17, Eric Isselee, 31, Jason Wilde, 15, Kirti Bhole, 25 (top), LGAndrade, 22 (top), Martins Vanags, 25 (bottom), Minh Do, 9, Mizanul Islam, 7, 9, 12–13, Nicola Pulham, 16 (bottom), Nynke van Holten, 28–29, Ola_Ill, 7, Oleksiichik, 25 (middle), photomaster, 18–19, Rita_Kochmarjova, cover, 23 (top), 32, SakSa, 16 (top), Sherry Sinclair, 22 (bottom)

CONTENTS

CHAPTER 1

Meet the PYGMY GOAT

A little goat stares up at a pile of wood. It's at least four times the goat's height. But the goat doesn't care. With a little burst, it begins to climb. It leaps from log to log. Two more goats follow behind it. It's a race to the top!

Time for Treats

Once at the top, the goats jump around. They spring from one side of the pile to another. Then they freeze. They see their owner. And she has food! The young goats bound down the wood pile. Now it's a race to their **trough**!

females = does

males = bucks

babies = kids

CHAPTER 2

A SPECIAL PET

Pygmy goats are playful little animals. They love to leap and climb. When they are not playing, they are often eating. They enjoy munching on grass and hay. Like cows, goats chew their **cud**. This helps them break down tough plants.

COMPARING SIZES

PYGMY GOAT
18 to 20 inches
(46 to 51 centimeters)
LABRADOR
RETRIEVER
21 to 25 inches
(53 to 64 cm)
50 to 60
POUNDS
(23 to 27 kilograms)
65 to 70
POUNDS
(30 to 32 kg)

These goats will also eat **invasive species.**

Living Lawn Mowers

These small goats came to the United States in the late 1950s. Some people keep them as pets. Others use them for their milk or as lawn mowers! If a lawn is hard to mow, owners can put their hungry goats to work.

WHERE PYGMY GOATS CAME FROM

EUROPE
ASIA
AFRICA
AUSTRALIA
ANTARCTICA

CHAPTER 3

Pygmy Goat FEATURES

Pygmy goats look a lot like regular goats. They have narrow faces, long ears, and rectangular **pupils**. Pygmy goats grow horns, and bucks have larger horns than does. Some owners remove their goats' horns when they are young.

A pygmy goats' horns keep growing their whole life. A new ring grows each year. The goat's age can be found by counting these rings.

PYGMY GOAT COLORS

gray

brown

black

Hair and Hooves

Pygmy goats have **coarse** hair. It's straight and can be many different colors. Some goats have markings and patterns. Goats shed their winter coats in the spring. Owners must brush their goats to help remove all the hair. Goats also have hooves that never stop growing. Owners must trim the hooves every 6 to 8 weeks.

white

PARTS OF A PYGMY GOAT

WIDESET EYES
LONG EARS
BEARD (males only)

CHAPTER 4

Caring for a PYGMY GOAT

Pygmy goats need plenty of outdoor space. They shouldn't be kept indoors. Their **pen** needs a shelter. These little animals are good at escaping. They need a strong fence to keep them out of trouble. They also need stuff to climb and play on. These goats like to have fun!

Each goat needs around 200 square feet (18.6 sq m). That's about as big as a 1-car garage.

POPULAR PET GOAT BREEDS

Boer Goat

Myotonic (Fainting) Goat

Nigerian Dwarf Goat

Nubian Goat

Food and Water

Pygmy goats always need a trough of fresh, clean water. When it comes to food, grass and hay are best. They can also eat goat **pellets**. Owners should limit the amount though. These goats can easily become overweight. Pygmy goats need to lick mineral blocks. These give the goats **nutrients**.

What Can Pygmy Goats Eat?

grass

hay

goat pellets

Special Care

Goats are herd animals. They shouldn't be kept alone. Most owners have two or more. Pygmy goats need a vet that specializes in goat care. Vets give shots and medicine, remove horns, and trim hooves. The extra care can cost more. Despite the work, people love these playful goats.

By the NUMBERS

10 to 15 YEARS

LIFE SPAN

4

Number of chambers a goat stomach has

More than

200

TOTAL NUMBER OF GOAT BREEDS

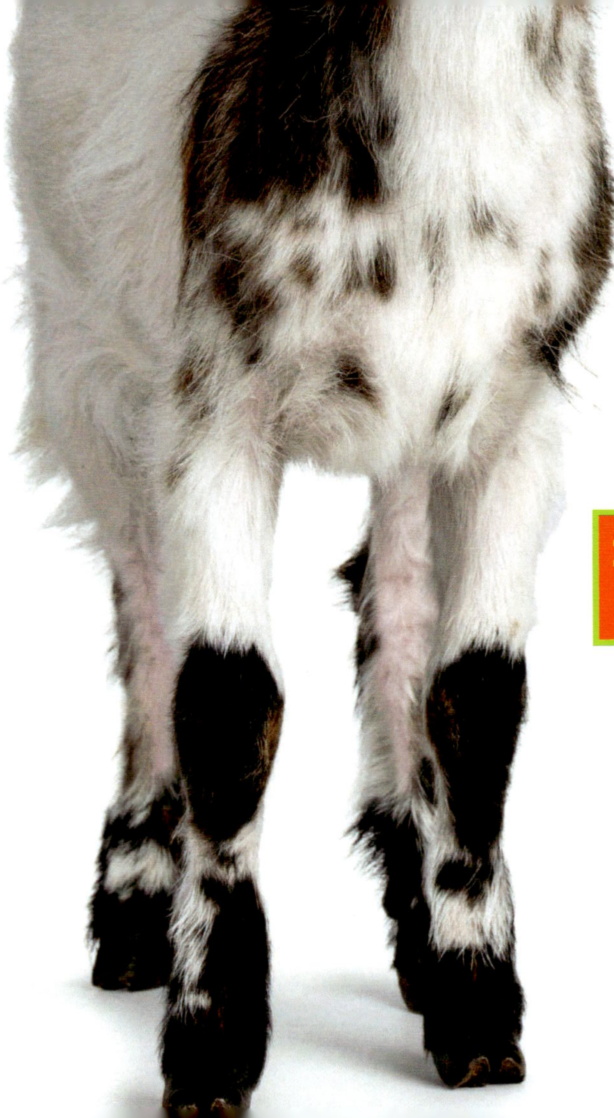

about

150

days

HOW LONG A DOE IS PREGNANT

GLOSSARY

coarse (KAWRS)—having a rough quality

cud (KUD)—food brought up into the mouth to be chewed again

invasive species (in-VEY-siv SPEE-seez)—animals that spread through an area where they are not native, often causing problems

nutrient (NYOO-tree-ent)—a substance or ingredient a person or animal needs to be healthy

pellet (PEL-it)—a small, hard ball of food

pen (PEN)—a small enclosed area for farm animals

pupil (PYU-pul)—the part of the eye that lets light in; in people, it's the round, black part of the eye

trough (TRAWF)—a long, shallow container from which animals eat or drink

BOOKS

Markovics, Joyce. *Incredible Goats*. Ann Arbor, MI: Cherry Lake Publishing, 2024.

Sabelko, Rebecca. *Goats*. Minneapolis: Bellwether Media, 2024.

WEBSITES

Pygmy Goat
www.lvzoo.org/animals/pygmy-goat/

Pygmy Goat
www.marylandzoo.org/animal/pygmy-goat/

INDEX